Words ABOUT Birds
of Aotearoa New Zealand

Geoffrey Fuller

SCHOLASTIC
AUCKLAND SYDNEY NEW YORK LONDON TORONTO
MEXICO CITY NEW DELHI HONG KONG

New Zealand is a land of birds,
from North to Stewart Island.
They are found in all the forests tall,
in parks and swamps and dry land.

Some birds seek their food at sea,
some find it on the land.
There are some that have long legs and bills
for finding food in sand.

Some birds are only seen at night,
while others like the sun.
But whichever bird it is,
we must protect each one.

Albatross / Toroa

The albatross can glide with ease
over southern storm-tossed seas.

It flies for miles on outstretched wings,
but never has been known to sing.

Bellbird / Korimako

In the spring
the bellbirds ring.

In summertime
you'll hear their chime.

When autumn's here
the bells ring clear.

In winter's chill
the bells are still.

Bittern / Matuku

Matuku, the bittern,
lives in swamps and bogs.
It eats a lot of slimy things,
like fish and eels and frogs.

It's very shy and secretive;
it hides its nest from sight.
The only way we know it's there
is its booming call at night.

Gannet / Tākapu

Of all the birds upon this planet,
few compare with the native gannet.
It hunts the sea for fishes edible;
its diving skills are quite incredible.

Godwit / Kuaka

Godwits fly from northern shores
to summer in our land.
They gather on the coastal flats,
and find their food in sand.

In winter they fly back again
and leave behind our coast.
It seems as if they can't decide
which land they like the most!

Gulls / Karoro & Akiaki

Wherever there is sand and sea,
or wharves and boats and hulls,
you'll see them fly, and hear the cry
of common native gulls.

Akiaki, the red-billed gull,
is grey and white, and smaller.
Karoro, the black-backed gull,
is black and white, and taller.

Harrier Hawk / Kāhu

The harrier hunts without a rest;
it flaps and glides, then glides and flaps.
It searches north, south, east and west,
and has no use at all for maps.

Kākāpō / Night Parrot

The kākāpō's a shy bird,
a parrot of the night.
Its home within the forest
is hidden out of sight.
If you wish to see it,
the places you must look
are far from town, in bushland
. . . or in a picture book!

Kea / Mountain Parrot

In southern mountain scenery
lives the cheeky kea.
It blends with forest greenery,
stealing people's food and gear.

When climbers go abseiling,
where there's ice and snow and skiers,
it'll be there, never failing,
the watchful mountain kea.

Kererū / Wood Pigeon

The native pigeon feeds on fruits,
berries, leaves and new green shoots.
A silent bird — it never sings —
the kererū flies on whistling wings.

Kiwi

The kiwi hunts for grubs at night,
it's shy and rarely seen,
but clever ornithologists
can tell where it has been.

The kiwi's not like other birds,
it shrieks instead of sings.
And it never tries to fly
. . . it has such little wings!

Mallard / Rakiraki

The mallard is a water bird,
a special kind of duck.
It feeds on grass and water weeds
and worms it finds in muck.
From pond bottoms and stream beds
it gobbles tasty snacks.
It swims, it flies, it waddles,
but when it sings – it quacks!

Ruru / Morepork

Ruru is the little owl
that comes out when it's dark.
You can hear it in the forest,
and sometimes in the park.

Nocturnal birds are hard to spot,
unless there is a moon.
But when you hear, "Morepork! Morepork!"
that is the ruru's tune.

Yellow-eyed Penguin / Hoiho

The penguin's not like other birds;
it never flies and never sings.
It spends a lot of time at sea,
and glides with flippers — not with wings.

Penguins catch a lot of fish
and have them for their dinner.
They have to keep on eating them
to stop from getting thinner!

Pūkeko / Swamp Hen

Pūkeko love the riverside
and places that are damp.
They feed on grubs and bugs and worms,
as through the swamps they tramp.

Sometimes found among the crops,
or foraging on farms,
pūkeko are a common bird,
and one with many charms.

Black and blue, a touch of green,
a flash of white beneath its tail,
with bill and legs both coloured red
. . . a truly handsome native rail.

Pied Shag / Kāruhiruhi

Native cormorants, or shags,
love to rest on rocks and crags.

Their bills have hooks to end their shape
so slippery fishes can't escape.

Pied Stilt / Poaka

It wades along the foreshore
among the stones and silt.
It's seeking big fat worms and crabs.
It's poaka, the stilt.

With long red legs and pointed bill,
it feeds when it's low tide.
You'll have no trouble seeing it;
it's black and white — it's pied!

Takahē / Notornis

Among the lakes and mountain passes,
takahē feed on tussock grasses.
Thought extinct for fifty years,
happily they reappeared.

Tūī / Parson Bird

The song of the tūī may be heard in
Northland, Southland, Westland, Auckland
. . . and in Whanganui.

The song of the tūī may be heard in
Wellington, Masterton, Palmerston, Hamilton
. . . and in Maunganui.

The song of the tūī may be heard in
Tauranga, Otorohanga, Raumahanga, OngaOnga
. . . and in Taumarunui.

The song of the tūī may be heard in
Timaru, Oamaru, Putāruru, Tokomaru
. . . and in Wingatui.

And ALL OVER Aotearoa New Zealand!

Moa

A giant bird, and quite distinct,
the moa, sadly, is extinct.
There is no chance that you will see 'em
. . . unless you go to a museum!

Geoffrey Francis Fuller (1925–2011) was educated at Rongotai Boys' College in Wellington before pursuing his love for art through Wellington Technical College and Canterbury University School of Art in Christchurch. In 1952 he graduated with a Diploma in Fine Arts in Painting, and trained as a teacher of Art at Auckland Teachers' College. He taught at four different secondary schools before eventually retiring as Head of Art in 1985.

A talented painter in oils, acrylics and watercolours, Geoffrey was regularly featured in exhibitions throughout Hawke's Bay, and has paintings in both private and public collections in New Zealand, USA, England, Japan, South Africa and Australia. He was lauded with many awards for his work, including, the Louise Lonsdale Prize for Life Drawing, the Queen Elizabeth II Art Award in 1966 and 1970, and the Norsewear Art Award in 1987.

During his life, Geoffrey completed numerous design commissions, including murals, stained-glass window designs, altar silverware, heraldic coats of arms, civic sculptures, and postage stamps. From his middle name, his wife and daughters dubbed him 'Saint Francis', after Saint Francis of Assisi, who shared his love for birds and nature.

This book was published in his memory.